UNVEILING ROOTS

TRACING AFRICAN AMERICAN ANCESTRY AND SLAVE RECORDS

Penelope Green

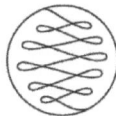

GLOBAL
PUBLISHING
SOLUTIONS

UNVEILING ROOTS: TRACING AFRICAN AMERICAN ANCESTRY AND SLAVE RECORDS by Penelope Green

Published by Global Publishing Solutions, LLC
923 Fieldside Drive
Matteson, Illinois 60443
www.globalpublishingsolutions.com

Library of Congress Control Number:
2023945627
International Standard Book Number
979-8-9886045-8-7
E-book International Standard Book Number:
979-8-9886045-9-4

Printed in the United States of America

TABLE OF CONTENTS

TABLE OF CONTENTS

INTRODUCTION: THE JOURNEY BEGINS - EMBRACING THE PAST TO SHAPE THE FUTURE

In the tapestry of time, our roots run deep, weaving a narrative of lives lived, dreams pursued, and struggles overcome. Each thread represents a story, a memory, an identity that has shaped us into who we are today. For African Americans seeking to trace their ancestry, this tapestry can sometimes appear fragmented, frayed by the weight of history's injustices. Yet, within the folds of the past, lies a journey of discovery that not only unveils personal heritage but also contributes to reshaping the future.

Welcome to the pages of "Unveiling Roots: Tracing African American Ancestry and Slave Records." Just as our first journey, "Tracing Roots: A Step-by-Step Guide to Discovering Your Ancestry," opened doors of exploration, this book embarks on a more intricate expedition—one that delves into the often obscured history of African American ancestors and the rich tapestry of their experiences. Our quest here is not just about understanding where we come from but also about embracing our heritage to influence where we're headed.

For too long, African American genealogy has been entwined with the struggle to reclaim identities erased by slavery and systematic marginalization. As we embark on this journey together, we'll navigate the complexities and sensitivities of tracing ancestry through slave records, plantation archives, and a historical landscape that can both enlighten and challenge us. We will explore the resilience and strength of individuals who lived through unimaginable trials, reminding us of the indomitable spirit that courses through our veins.

In the chapters ahead, we'll uncover a treasure trove of resources and strategies designed to guide you through every step of your ancestral journey. We'll unearth stories buried deep within plantation journals, letters, and diaries, turning the pages of history to reconstruct narratives long silenced. We'll decipher census data and vital records, piecing together the puzzle of our lineage. And we'll embrace the revelations offered by modern genetics, illuminating our connections to the past and each other.

"Unveiling Roots" recognizes that genealogy is more than just a study of names and dates; it is a testament to the lives lived and the legacies left behind. As you embark on this journey, remember that each discovery you make, every story you unveil, becomes a bridge between generations. By preserving these stories, you honor the struggles and triumphs of those who paved the way for your existence.

As we navigate the intricacies of African American genealogy and delve into the often poignant stories woven into the fabric of our heritage, remember that you are not alone on this path. Through the pages of this book, you will find guidance, inspiration, and a community of fellow seekers. Together, we will embrace the past to shape a future that celebrates the diversity, strength, and resilience of our African American heritage.

So let the journey begin—a journey that will unearth treasures of knowledge, forge connections across time, and empower you to honor the past as you shape the story of tomorrow.

THE UNIQUE CHALLENGES AND RICH REWARDS OF TRACING AFRICAN AMERICAN ANCESTRY

Introduction

The quest to uncover one's ancestral roots is a journey of profound significance, a pilgrimage into the past that holds the power to shape our understanding of the present and future. For African Americans, this journey is often fraught with unique challenges and intricacies that reflect a history marked by both resilience and adversity. In this chapter, we will explore the distinctive obstacles and the invaluable rewards that accompany the pursuit of African American genealogy.

Challenges in African American Genealogy: Navigating the Shadows of History

Tracing African American ancestry differs from other genealogical pursuits due to the profound impact of slavery and its aftermath. The institution of slavery disrupted familial ties, erased identities, and subjected millions to a system that dehumanized and marginalized. As a result, the path to discovering one's lineage can be obscured by lost records, fragmented family connections, and a legacy of systemic discrimination. Some of the challenges include:

1. **Scarcity of Records**: The systematic denial of education, ownership, and legal rights to enslaved individuals often meant that they left behind scant records. Births, marriages, and deaths were seldom documented, making it difficult to establish family connections.

2. **Fragmented Family Histories**: Slavery forced families apart through sale, separation, or displacement, creating a disconnect between generations. Reconstructing lineages and finding connections across these fractures can be an intricate puzzle.

3. **Name Changes**: Many enslaved individuals were given names by their owners, erasing their original names and cultural identities. These names might have changed multiple times due to transfers of ownership.

4. **Lack of Civil Rights**: Even after emancipation, African Americans faced barriers in accessing education, voting, and property ownership. This limited their presence in official records and documentation.

5. **Prejudice and Discrimination**: Racial biases have led to the omission or misrepresentation of African Americans in historical records, further complicating the research process.

Rewards of Tracing African American Ancestry: Connecting to Identity and Resilience

Despite these challenges, the journey of African American genealogy is rich with rewards that extend far beyond the realms of documentation. By delving into the past, individuals have the opportunity to:

1. **Reclaim Identity**: Unearthing the names, stories, and experiences of ancestors helps restore a sense of identity that was deliberately suppressed. It allows us to reconnect with cultural heritage and traditions.

2. **Honor Resilience**: The stories of enslaved individuals and their descendants are stories of triumph over adversity. By tracing these stories, we pay homage to the strength and determination that has been passed down through generations.

3. **Forge Connections**: The journey often brings families together, reuniting branches separated by time and circumstance. It also fosters a sense of community among African Americans who share a common history.

4. **Educate Future Generations**: As we piece together our past, we create a legacy for future generations. Understanding the struggles and successes of our ancestors

inspires a sense of purpose and resilience in our children and grandchildren.

5. **Contribute to History**: By uncovering hidden stories, we enrich the broader narrative of American history. We shed light on the lives of those who were marginalized and contribute to a more complete understanding of the nation's past.

The journey to trace African American ancestry requires patience, tenacity, and a deep respect for the past. It is an acknowledgment of the challenges faced by our forebears and a celebration of the resilience that courses through our veins. As we move forward in this exploration, remember that each piece of information, each connection made, is a step toward a greater understanding of who we are and a testament to the enduring spirit of our ancestors.

BUILDING A STRONG FOUNDATION: GATHERING FAMILY STORIES, ORAL HISTORIES, AND TRADITIONS

Introduction

At the heart of every family's history lie stories—fragments of the past passed down through generations, weaving a tapestry of memories, emotions, and experiences. For African Americans seeking to trace their roots, these stories serve as a crucial foundation for navigating a history marked by complexities. In this chapter, we will delve into the art of gathering family stories, oral histories, and traditions, creating a bridge between the past and the present.

The Power of Family Stories: Unveiling Hidden Treasures

Family stories are the bedrock upon which genealogy research is built. They provide insights into personal experiences, cultural practices, and historical events that have shaped generations. As you embark on this journey, consider these steps to uncover and preserve these invaluable stories:

1. **Engage with Elders**: Elders within your family are reservoirs of wisdom and memories. Take the time to sit

down with them, ask open-ended questions, and listen attentively as they recount tales of their youth, their parents, and their grandparents.

2. **Capture Oral Histories**: Recording oral histories is a powerful way to preserve firsthand accounts. Use audio or video recordings to capture the nuances of voices and emotions. Prepare a list of questions that encourage storytelling, touching on topics like family migrations, celebrations, challenges, and pivotal life moments.

3. **Document Traditions and Customs**: Family traditions, rituals, and customs carry cultural significance that can provide valuable clues to your ancestry. Whether it's recipes, songs, or annual celebrations, document these practices and learn about their origins.

4. **Cross-Reference Stories**: Compare stories from different family members to identify common threads and discrepancies. Sometimes, the same event may be remembered differently by various individuals, providing opportunities for deeper exploration.

Challenges in Gathering Family Stories

While family stories hold a wealth of information, it's essential to approach this endeavor with sensitivity and awareness of potential challenges:

1. **Silences and Gaps**: Due to the impact of historical trauma, some family stories might be painful or difficult to discuss. Approach these conversations with empathy, understanding that not all stories may be shared openly.

2. **Fading Memories**: As time passes, memories fade, and details may become less accurate. Documenting stories as soon as possible helps ensure their accuracy and preserves the voices of those who hold them.

3. **Lost Histories**: The disruption caused by slavery and migration can lead to lost histories, where certain details or branches of the family tree remain obscured. This is a reminder of the importance of cherishing the stories that are still within reach.

Preserving and Sharing Family Stories

Once you've gathered family stories and oral histories, it's important to take steps to preserve and share them:

1. **Create a Repository**: Organize recordings, photographs, and documents in a safe and accessible place. Consider creating digital backups to prevent loss.

2. **Transcribe and Translate**: If interviews are conducted in languages other than English, transcribe and translate them to ensure the content is understood by future generations.

3. **Share with Family**: Share the gathered stories with your extended family. This fosters a sense of connection and ensures that the narratives are passed down to subsequent generations.

4. **Include Context**: Provide context for the stories by referencing historical events, cultural practices, and geographical locations. This enriches the understanding of both the storyteller and the audience.

As you journey through the treasure trove of family stories and oral histories, remember that you are not only connecting with your past but also preserving a legacy for the future. By cherishing these narratives, you weave a stronger bond between generations and honor the resilience and wisdom of those who came before you.

ESSENTIAL GENEALOGY RESEARCH TOOLS AND TECHNIQUES FOR AFRICAN AMERICAN FAMILIES

Introduction

In the quest to uncover the hidden threads of African American ancestry, research tools and techniques are the compass that guides us through the labyrinth of history. With the knowledge of where to search and how to interpret the available resources, you can navigate the challenges and piece together a more complete picture of your family's past. In this chapter, we'll explore the essential tools and techniques that form the foundation of successful African American genealogical research.

Building Your Research Toolkit

1. **Online Databases and Archives**: The digital age has brought vast collections of historical records to your fingertips. Explore websites dedicated to genealogy, like Ancestry.com, FamilySearch.org, and African American-focused databases such as the African American Genealogical Research Center.
2. **Local and State Archives**: Visit local and state archives to access vital records, land deeds, wills, and other documents.

Some areas have records specifically related to African American history and communities.

3. **Historical Societies and Libraries**: Many historical societies and libraries maintain collections that can aid your research. Seek out those with an emphasis on African American history or the history of the region where your ancestors lived.

4. **Slave Narratives and Oral Histories**: Slave narratives, recorded during the 1930s as part of the Federal Writers' Project, offer firsthand accounts of life during slavery. These narratives, along with family oral histories, can provide unique insights.

5. **Church Records**: Church records often document births, marriages, and deaths, offering valuable genealogical information. Look for churches that were central to your ancestors' communities.

Effective Research Techniques

1. **Start with What You Know**: Begin your research with the information you have about your immediate family. Document names, birth dates, and locations as accurately as possible.

2. **Work Backwards in Time**: Start with more recent records and progressively move further back in time. This helps ensure accuracy and allows you to build a solid foundation.

3. **Use the FAN Club Principle**: The Friends, Associates, and Neighbors (FAN) Club principle involves researching the extended community around your ancestors. Sometimes, indirect connections can lead to breakthroughs.

4. **Cluster Research**: Study the individuals and families who lived near your ancestors. This can provide context and uncover potential relationships.

5. **DNA Testing**: Consider DNA testing to supplement your research. DNA can reveal distant relatives, ethnic origins, and connections you might not find through traditional records.

Navigating Records with Sensitivity

1. **Language and Terminology**: Be aware of the historical terminology used in records, including racial slurs and outdated terms. This awareness helps you interpret documents more accurately.

2. **Record Variations**: Spelling variations of names were common, especially due to literacy rates among African Americans during certain periods. Be prepared to explore different spellings of names.

3. **Interpreting Plantation Records**: When examining plantation records, approach them with empathy and sensitivity. These records may contain details about enslaved individuals, such as names, ages, and skills.
4. **Contextual Understanding**: Understand the historical context of the time in which your ancestors lived. Laws, customs, and societal norms significantly impact the records you encounter.

As you delve into genealogical research, remember that each document you unearth, each connection you make, brings you one step closer to understanding your family's history. The journey might have twists and turns, but armed with these essential tools and techniques, you are equipped to navigate the complexities and unveil the stories of your ancestors.

TRIBAL IDENTITY AND ANCESTRAL - THE SIGNIFICANCE OF SLAVE RECORDS: UNDERSTANDING THEIR IMPORTANCE IN GENEALOGY RESEARCH

Introduction

In the landscape of African American genealogy, slave records stand as both profound artifacts and poignant testaments to a history marked by suffering and resilience. These records hold a key to unlocking hidden stories, tracing lineages, and connecting with the struggles and triumphs of our ancestors. In this chapter, we delve into the significance of slave records and their role in shaping our understanding of the past.

Unveiling the Voices of the Enslaved

Slave records, while often somber, provide an invaluable window into the lives of those who were historically marginalized and silenced. These documents encompass a range of information, including:

1. **Slave Registers**: Registers of enslaved individuals kept by slave owners, providing details such as names, ages, physical descriptions, and sometimes familial relationships.

2. **Bill of Sales and Property Records**: Documentation of enslaved individuals being bought or sold, shedding light on their movement between owners and locations.

3. **Plantation Ledgers**: Records of daily life on plantations, including tasks assigned to enslaved individuals, births, deaths, and punishments administered.

4. **Runaway Slave Advertisements**: Advertisements seeking the return of escaped slaves, which may include descriptions, skills, and personal anecdotes.

Importance of Slave Records in Genealogy Research

1. **Establishing Connections**: Slave records can help establish familial connections that were often disrupted by the horrors of slavery. Names, ages, and familial references provide crucial clues for building family trees.

2. **Reconstructing Lineages**: By piecing together various slave records, you can trace family lines across generations, illuminating the paths that led to your present existence.

3. **Humanizing Ancestors**: These records offer glimpses into the personalities, skills, and experiences of the enslaved, humanizing them beyond the dehumanizing institutions they endured.

4. **Discovering Origins**: Some records may hint at places of origin or ethnic backgrounds, contributing to a more comprehensive understanding of your ancestral heritage.

5. **Cultural Insights**: Plantation records reveal cultural practices, traditions, and even instances of resistance that provide insight into the resilience of African American communities.

Navigating the Emotional Terrain

While slave records provide valuable insights, they often evoke complex emotions due to the suffering endured by enslaved individuals. Approach this research with sensitivity:

1. **Acknowledging Emotions**: It's normal to feel a mix of emotions while exploring these records, including sadness, anger, and empathy. Allow yourself to process these feelings as you uncover the stories.

2. **Balancing Hope and Pain**: While many records reveal harsh realities, they also offer glimpses of triumph and resistance. Balancing these narratives can provide a more holistic perspective.

3. **Honoring Their Stories**: Viewing slave records as a means of honoring the lives and stories of the enslaved can help contextualize your research in a meaningful way.

As you navigate the world of slave records, remember that your efforts contribute to a broader narrative that aims to shed light on the lives of those who were often left in the shadows of history. By embracing these records and the stories they reveal, you ensure that the resilience and strength of your ancestors are remembered and celebrated for generations to come.

NAVIGATING PLANTATION ARCHIVES: HOW TO ACCESS AND INTERPRET SLAVE-RELATED

Introduction

Plantation archives hold a wealth of historical documents that offer a glimpse into the lives of the enslaved and the environments they navigated. These archives house records that range from account books to personal diaries, and decoding them can provide valuable insights into the experiences of your ancestors. In this chapter, we will explore the methods for accessing and interpreting plantation archives to uncover the hidden stories of African American families.

Gaining Access to Plantation Archives

1. **Local Libraries and Archives**: Research the archives and libraries in the areas where your ancestors lived. Many contain documents related to local plantations, landowners, and historical events.
2. **Historical Societies**: Reach out to historical societies in the regions of interest. They may maintain archives, documents, and resources related to plantations and their inhabitants.
3. **University Collections**: Universities and research institutions often house extensive archives related to local

history, including plantation records. These resources might be accessible through on-site visits or online databases.

4. **Online Resources**: Some digitized plantation archives are accessible online. Look for websites of historical organizations, libraries, and universities that share their collections digitally.

Interpreting Plantation Records

1. **Account Books and Ledgers**: These documents might record transactions involving the enslaved, such as purchases, sales, and provisions. Details of clothing, food, and medical care can provide insights into daily life.

2. **Diaries and Letters**: Personal writings of plantation owners and overseers may contain references to the enslaved individuals working on the plantation. These can offer glimpses into their lives and relationships.

3. **Inventories**: Estate inventories taken after a landowner's death often list enslaved individuals by name, along with brief descriptions and sometimes monetary values.

4. **Plantation Journals**: Journals kept by those who lived on or visited plantations can provide context for the social dynamics and events that unfolded.

Navigating Ethical Considerations

1. **Respect and Empathy**: Approach plantation records with a deep sense of respect and empathy for the lives they document. Remember that these documents represent real individuals who lived through challenging circumstances.

2. **Acknowledging Power Dynamics**: Recognize the inherent power dynamics in these records. Understand that they were often created by those in positions of privilege and might present a skewed perspective.

3. **Balancing Awareness and Emotional Well-being**: Delving into plantation archives can be emotionally challenging. Pace yourself and seek support if needed to navigate the potential emotional toll.

Documenting and Sharing Your Discoveries

1. **Transcriptions and Annotations**: As you decipher handwriting and interpret documents, transcribe them into legible text and provide annotations for context.

2. **Citation and Preservation**: Accurately cite the sources of your findings and consider contributing to the preservation

of historical records by sharing your findings with relevant institutions.

3. **Family and Community**: Share your discoveries with your family and the broader African American genealogical community. Collaborate with others who might be researching the same plantation or region.

By delving into plantation archives, you honor the resilience and contributions of your ancestors while shedding light on the complexities of their lives. Each document you interpret adds depth to the narrative of African American history and helps ensure that the voices of the enslaved are heard and remembered.

UNEARTHING STORIES FROM PLANTATION JOURNALS, LETTERS, AND DIARIES

Introduction

In the pages of plantation journals, letters, and diaries, lie the echoes of the past, the intimate thoughts and observations of those who lived in an era marked by profound social change. These personal documents provide a unique lens through which we can view the lives of both the enslaved and those who held power. In this chapter, we will embark on a journey to unearthing stories from these evocative records and understanding the lives they illuminate.

The Rich Tapestry of Personal Records

1. **Plantation Journals**: These chronicles often contain daily observations, weather reports, and events on the plantation. They might also mention interactions with the enslaved, providing insights into their work, relationships, and struggles.

2. **Letters and Correspondence**: Personal letters exchanged between plantation owners, family members, and friends can unveil candid conversations about daily life, emotions, and sometimes insights into the lives of the enslaved.

3. **Diaries and Personal Writings**: Private thoughts, reflections, and accounts of events find their way into diaries. These writings offer glimpses into personal experiences and perspectives.

Key Themes to Explore

1. **Relationships**: Look for clues about interactions between the enslaved and the landowners or overseers. These relationships could reveal dynamics of power, dependency, or even unexpected alliances.
2. **Work and Daily Life**: Through these records, you can piece together details about the tasks, routines, and challenges faced by the enslaved individuals on the plantation.
3. **Cultural Practices**: Journals and letters might mention celebrations, ceremonies, and traditions practiced by both the landowners and the enslaved, giving insight into cultural exchanges and influences.
4. **Resistance and Agency**: Occasionally, personal records contain hints of resistance, whether through subtle actions or overt defiance, providing a glimpse into the resilience of the oppressed.

Interpreting Personal Records

1. **Contextual Reading**: Understand the broader historical context in which these records were written. This helps decipher the motivations behind the entries and the possible biases of the authors.

2. **Reading Between the Lines**: Sometimes, the most revealing details are not explicitly stated. Pay attention to silences, omissions, and what is left unsaid.

3. **Comparative Analysis**: Compare different sources to cross-reference information and corroborate details. Sometimes, multiple perspectives shed light on the same event.

Navigating Complex Narratives

1. **Multiple Perspectives**: Remember that the viewpoints presented in these documents might be skewed by the perspectives of their authors. Try to triangulate information with other sources.

2. **Balancing Emotions**: Personal records can evoke emotional responses due to the content they contain. Approach them with a sense of empathy while maintaining objectivity.

Preserving and Sharing Your Discoveries

1. **Digital Preservation**: If possible, digitize the records you discover to ensure their preservation and accessibility for future generations.

2. **Annotation and Analysis**: Provide context through annotations, explaining historical references and the significance of events.

3. **Educational Sharing**: Share your findings with educational institutions, historical societies, and online communities to contribute to the collective understanding of African American history.

By unearthing stories from plantation journals, letters, and diaries, you immerse yourself in the lived experiences of individuals who shaped and were shaped by a tumultuous era. These records offer a more intimate glimpse into the past, allowing us to connect with the humanity of those who navigated the complexities of their time.

THE POWER OF CENSUS DATA: TRACING ANCESTRY THROUGH CHANGING DEMOGRAPHICS

Introduction

Census data stands as a cornerstone of genealogy research, providing snapshots of societies at different points in time. For African American families, census records offer a unique opportunity to trace lineage, understand changing demographics, and uncover historical context. In this chapter, we will delve into the power of census data and how it can illuminate your ancestry.

Census Records: A Historical Portrait

1. **Evolution of Census**: The U.S. federal census has been conducted decennially since 1790, providing a comprehensive record of households, demographics, occupations, and more.

2. **Key Information**: Census records contain essential details such as names, ages, birthplaces, family relationships, occupations, and, in later years, even educational levels.

3. **Enumeration of Enslaved Individuals**: Prior to 1870, enslaved individuals were often recorded only by age, gender, and status. However, post-1870, they were listed by name, providing an important shift in visibility.

Tracing Ancestry Through Census Records

1. **Decade-by-Decade Exploration**: Begin with the most recent census and work your way backward. Each census unveils a snapshot of your family's circumstances at a specific point in time.
2. **Analyze Changes**: As you follow your family through multiple censuses, observe changes in family size, locations, occupations, and other relevant details. These changes can indicate migrations and transitions.
3. **Comparative Analysis**: Compare census records with other sources, such as family stories and documents, to verify information and piece together a comprehensive picture.

Understanding Historical Context

1. **Social and Economic Trends**: Census data reflects larger social and economic trends that might have impacted your

ancestors' lives. Economic depressions, wars, and societal changes are all reflected in these records.

2. **Migration Patterns**: Tracking your family's movement through different census years can reveal migration patterns, helping you understand why your ancestors relocated.

3. **Community Insights**: Census data offers insights into the communities your ancestors lived in, including neighbors, ethnic compositions, and neighborhood dynamics.

Challenges and Considerations

1. **Name Variations**: Census records might contain name variations due to transcription errors, accents, or changes in spelling. Be prepared to explore different spellings.

2. **Ages and Birth Years**: Ages listed in census records might not be entirely accurate. Use approximate birth years and cross-reference with other records for consistency.

3. **Misclassifications**: Some individuals might have been misclassified racially, affecting the accuracy of information related to your African American ancestors.

Preserving and Sharing Insights

1. **Document Your Findings**: Keep detailed notes about the information you discover in census records, including which census year you accessed and any discrepancies you encounter.
2. **Share with Family**: Share your findings with your family to foster a deeper understanding of your collective history.
3. **Contribute to Research**: Participate in collaborative genealogy efforts by contributing your insights to online databases and community projects.

By harnessing the power of census data, you not only trace your own lineage but also contribute to the broader narrative of African American history. These records offer a tangible link to the past, allowing you to visualize the lives of your ancestors and their journey through changing demographics.

VITAL RECORDS UNVEILED: BIRTH, MARRIAGE, AND DEATH CERTIFICATES AS GENEALOGICAL CLUES

Vital records, including birth, marriage, and death certificates, are the bedrock of genealogical research, providing crucial information that anchors your ancestors within historical timelines. For African American families, these records can offer valuable insights into lineage, family connections, and life milestones. In this chapter, we will explore the significance of vital records and how they can unlock hidden stories of your ancestors.

Understanding Vital Records

1. **Birth Certificates**: Birth records document an individual's birth date, place of birth, and parentage. For African Americans, birth certificates become vital links to understanding generations that were often underrepresented in historical records.

2. **Marriage Certificates**: Marriage records record the union of individuals, including names, dates of marriage, and sometimes the names of parents. These records offer glimpses into relationships and societal norms of the time.

3. **Death Certificates**: Death records provide information about an individual's date of death, cause of death, and sometimes burial location. These documents offer insights into family structures and health conditions.

Navigating Birth Records

1. **Access and Availability**: Birth records might be housed at the county or state level. Availability varies by location and the time period in question.
2. **Delayed Birth Certificates**: Some African Americans might have obtained delayed birth certificates due to lack of initial documentation, providing an alternative source of birth information.
3. **Cross-Reference with Census Data**: Cross-referencing birth records with census data can verify the accuracy of birth dates and family relationships.

Unveiling Marital Connections

1. **Marriage Records as Milestones**: Marriage records mark significant life events and provide insight into societal norms, age at marriage, and family relationships.

2. **Marriage Registers**: Local churches often maintain marriage registers that document ceremonies, offering an additional source for marriage details.
3. **Cross-Reference with Other Records**: Compare marriage records with census data and other sources to corroborate information and build a comprehensive narrative.

Death Records and Family Insights

1. **Family Connections**: Death records often list the names of parents, revealing familial relationships that can be instrumental in constructing family trees.
2. **Cause of Death**: Understanding causes of death can provide context for historical health challenges and societal conditions.
3. **Burial Information**: Burial locations listed in death records can lead to cemetery records or headstones that provide further genealogical information.

Challenges and Considerations

1. **Name Variations**: Like other records, vital records might contain name variations that can make identification challenging.

2. **Incomplete or Missing Records**: Some vital records might be incomplete or missing due to historical circumstances. Look for alternative sources or indirect clues.

3. **Privacy Restrictions**: Access to more recent vital records might be restricted due to privacy laws. Be aware of time restrictions on accessing certain records.

Documenting and Sharing Discoveries

1. **Record Citations**: Accurately cite the sources of your findings for future reference and verification.

2. **Share with Family**: Share the information you uncover with your family members to foster a deeper understanding of your shared heritage.

3. **Contribute to Databases**: Consider contributing your findings to online genealogy databases to help other researchers.

Vital records are windows into the intimate details of your ancestors' lives, allowing you to witness their birth, marriage, and passing. By delving into these records, you breathe life into their stories and honor the moments that shaped your family's history.

EMBRACING DNA: TRACING AFRICAN AMERICAN ANCESTRY THROUGH GENETIC CONNECTIONS

The advent of DNA testing has revolutionized genealogical research, offering an unprecedented opportunity to uncover ancestral connections and heritage. For African American families, DNA testing holds the promise of bridging gaps left by historical records, providing insights into ancestral origins and distant relatives. In this chapter, we will explore the power of DNA testing in tracing African American ancestry.

The Science of DNA Testing

1. **Types of DNA**: Autosomal DNA, Y-DNA, and mitochondrial DNA are the primary types of DNA tests used for genealogical research, each offering unique insights into different aspects of ancestry.
2. **Autosomal DNA**: Autosomal DNA tests analyze the mixture of genetic material from both parents, providing insights into recent and more distant family connections.

3. **Y-DNA**: Y-DNA tests trace the direct paternal line, passing from father to son, providing information about the direct male lineage.

4. **Mitochondrial DNA**: Mitochondrial DNA tests trace the maternal line, passing from mother to all her children, regardless of gender.

Tracing African American Ancestry Through DNA

1. **Ethnic Origins**: DNA testing can reveal ethnic breakdowns, shedding light on ancestral regions and contributing to a deeper understanding of heritage.

2. **Genetic Matches**: DNA databases connect you with individuals who share segments of DNA, potentially leading to the discovery of relatives and extended family.

3. **Breakthroughs in Brick Walls**: DNA testing can break through genealogical "brick walls" by identifying previously unknown relatives and connections.

Navigating the Complexities of African American DNA

1. **Admixture and Migration**: African American DNA often reveals a diverse mix of ethnicities due to historical

migrations, including African, European, and Native American roots.

2. **Shared Ancestry**: Connecting with DNA matches may reveal shared ancestors or common geographical origins, helping you piece together your family's history.

Ethical Considerations and Emotional Impact

1. **Informed Consent**: Consider the implications of DNA testing for privacy and informed consent. Ensure you understand how your genetic data will be used.

2. **Ethical Exploration**: Some DNA results might reveal unexpected family connections or challenge long-held beliefs. Approach these revelations with sensitivity.

Integration with Traditional Research

1. **Complementary Research**: DNA testing should be integrated with traditional genealogical research to create a comprehensive family history.

2. **Support from Experts**: Consult genealogy experts, genetic counselors, and community resources to help you interpret and navigate your DNA results.

Preserving and Sharing Your DNA Findings

1. **Educate and Share**: Educate your family members about the power of DNA testing and share your findings to encourage a broader understanding of your shared heritage.
2. **Contribute to Databases**: Contribute your DNA results to databases and projects that aim to map the genetic landscape of African American ancestry.

DNA testing opens a new avenue of exploration in the journey to trace African American ancestry. It connects you with a vast network of individuals who share fragments of your genetic heritage, providing insights that extend beyond the written records of history. By embracing DNA testing, you embrace the threads that weave you into the intricate tapestry of humanity.

TELLING YOUR FAMILY'S STORY: WEAVING ANCESTRAL DISCOVERIES INTO A RICH TAPESTRY

As you journey through the intricate paths of African American genealogy, you accumulate a treasure trove of stories, records, and insights that paint a vivid portrait of your family's history. In this final chapter, we explore the art of weaving these ancestral discoveries into a compelling narrative, preserving your family's legacy for generations to come.

Crafting a Narrative of Resilience and Identity

1. **Narrative Arc**: Create a structured narrative that guides readers through the generations, highlighting key individuals, pivotal moments, and the overarching themes that define your family's journey.
2. **Personal Insights**: Infuse your narrative with personal insights and reflections, sharing your own emotions and discoveries as you unraveled the past.

Incorporating Various Sources of Information

1. **Diverse Voices**: Integrate oral histories, written records, DNA findings, and other sources to offer a multi-dimensional view of your family's history.

2. **Visual Elements**: Incorporate photographs, maps, and documents to visually illustrate the lives and times of your ancestors.

Exploring Cultural Context and Heritage

1. **Historical Context**: Place your family's story within the broader context of African American history, highlighting social, political, and cultural influences that shaped their lives.

2. **Cultural Traditions**: Detail cultural practices, traditions, and values that have been passed down through generations, connecting your family to its roots.

Celebrating Resilience and Achievements

1. **Triumphs Over Adversity**: Showcase instances of resilience, determination, and achievement that reveal the strength and spirit of your ancestors.

2. **Individual Stories**: Spotlight individual family members who played significant roles in shaping the family's

narrative, whether through entrepreneurship, education, activism, or other pursuits.

Preserving the Past for the Future

1. **Documentation**: Keep detailed records of your research methods, findings, and sources. This documentation ensures the accuracy and credibility of your work.
2. **Digital Archiving**: Store your research digitally to safeguard against loss or damage. Regularly back up your data to multiple locations.

Sharing Your Family's Story

1. **Family Reunions**: Share your research findings at family gatherings, fostering a sense of connection and shared heritage.
2. **Online Platforms**: Consider creating a website, blog, or social media page to share your family's story with a broader audience.
3. **Genealogical Societies**: Join local or online genealogical societies to connect with others who share an interest in African American genealogy.

Legacy and Continuation

1. **Educational Initiatives**: Use your research to educate younger generations about their heritage, instilling a sense of pride and connection.

2. **Encourage Further Research**: Inspire other family members to continue the research journey, ensuring that the legacy of discovery endures.

As you weave the threads of your family's past into a rich tapestry, you breathe life into the stories of those who came before you. Your dedication to uncovering the hidden narratives of African American ancestry preserves the legacy of resilience, determination, and triumph. By sharing your family's story, you empower future generations to continue the exploration of their roots and to celebrate the vibrant mosaic of their heritage.

CONTINUING THE JOURNEY: RESOURCES, COMMUNITY, AND FUTURE EXPLORATIONS

Your journey through African American genealogy is not just a solitary pursuit—it's a thread woven into a broader tapestry of shared history and collective discovery. In this chapter, we'll explore the resources, communities, and avenues that can continue to support and enrich your exploration of African American ancestry into the future.

Embracing Lifelong Learning

1. **Stay Curious**: Genealogy is an ever-evolving field. Stay open to learning about new research techniques, tools, and historical insights.
2. **Continued Research**: As you gather more information, revisit and update your research periodically to incorporate new findings.

Genealogy Organizations and Communities

1. **Local Genealogical Societies**: Join local genealogy societies to connect with fellow researchers and access resources specific to your region.

2. **Online Forums and Groups**: Participate in online genealogy forums and social media groups focused on African American genealogy. Engage with others to share insights and ask questions.

Digital Repositories and Archives

1. **Digitized Collections**: Continuously explore online databases, digital archives, and repositories for new records that may have become available.
2. **Collaborative Projects**: Contribute to collaborative efforts to transcribe, index, or digitize records, making them more accessible for future researchers.

DNA and Genetic Genealogy

1. **Ongoing Testing**: DNA testing continues to advance. Consider periodically updating your DNA results to benefit from new discoveries.
2. **Genetic Genealogy Communities**: Engage with DNA-related forums and projects to connect with others who share genetic connections.

Cultural and Historical Institutions

1. **Museums and Cultural Centers**: Visit museums and centers dedicated to African American history to deepen your understanding of the cultural context of your ancestors.

2. **Archives and Libraries**: Continue to explore physical archives and libraries, as they may unveil hidden records that are yet to be digitized.

Educational Initiatives and Outreach

1. **Sharing with Schools**: Collaborate with local schools to offer educational sessions about African American genealogy, encouraging younger generations to connect with their heritage.

2. **Workshops and Webinars**: Attend workshops, webinars, and conferences focused on genealogy research, expanding your knowledge base and networking opportunities.

Documenting and Preserving Your Journey

1. **Organizational Systems**: Maintain well-organized digital and physical folders to ensure your research remains accessible and easy to navigate.

2. **Writing and Publishing**: Consider writing articles or books about your genealogical journey to inspire others and contribute to the collective knowledge.

Passing the Torch

1. **Engage the Younger Generation**: Encourage children and grandchildren to participate in family history research, ensuring the continuity of your legacy.
2. **Mentoring and Sharing**: Offer your expertise to newer genealogists, guiding them on their own journeys of discovery.

As you continue your journey through African American genealogy, remember that your efforts contribute to a broader narrative that honors the resilience, strength, and contributions of those who came before. The discoveries you make enrich not only your own understanding but also the collective understanding of African American history. Embrace the connections, resources, and communities available to you, and look to the future with the excitement of uncovering even more hidden stories and ancestral threads.

REFLECTIONS AND BEYOND: EMBRACING THE EVER-UNFOLDING STORY OF YOUR ANCESTRY

As you approach the end of this genealogical journey, take a moment to reflect on the profound impact it has had on your understanding of your African American heritage. This final chapter invites you to contemplate the significance of your discoveries, the connections you've forged, and the limitless potential for continued exploration of your ancestral story.

A Journey of Connection

1. **Rediscovering Heritage**: Reflect on how your journey has reconnected you with the stories, traditions, and cultural roots that are woven into your family's tapestry.
2. **Humanizing the Past**: Consider how your research has breathed life into names on records, transforming them into real people with emotions, dreams, and experiences.

Embracing Complexity

1. **Tributes to Resilience**: Recognize the strength and resilience of your ancestors in the face of adversity, and how their stories have shaped your identity.

2. **Navigating Contradictions**: Acknowledge that ancestral narratives can be complex, often blending stories of triumph and struggle, and how this complexity contributes to a richer understanding.

The Legacy of Discovery

1. **Educational Gifts**: Reflect on how your findings can serve as educational tools, teaching younger generations about their roots and inspiring them to explore their history.
2. **Community Contribution**: Contemplate the impact of your research on the larger African American genealogical community, and how your contributions have added to the collective knowledge.

Remaining Curious

1. **Unanswered Questions**: Embrace the realization that genealogy is a journey without a fixed endpoint. Some questions may remain unanswered, leaving room for future exploration.
2. **Continued Learning**: Consider how your journey has ignited a lifelong passion for learning, history, and the ever-evolving field of genealogy.

Passing on the Torch

1. **Inspiring Others**: Reflect on the possibility of inspiring others, both within your family and beyond, to embark on their own journeys of ancestral discovery.
2. **Legacy of Storytelling**: Recognize that the stories you've uncovered can be shared through generations, ensuring that the voices of your ancestors endure.

Gratitude and Appreciation

1. **Honoring the Past**: Take a moment to honor the sacrifices, achievements, and contributions of your ancestors that have paved the way for your present.
2. **Appreciating the Present**: Express gratitude for the opportunities and resources that allowed you to unearth the hidden narratives of your family history.

Continuing the Unfolding Story

As you close this chapter, remember that your genealogical journey is not truly ending—it's merely evolving. The story of your African American ancestry is boundless, with countless layers waiting to be discovered by future generations. Embrace the ever-unfolding narrative, keep your heart open to new insights, and celebrate the intricate mosaic of identities and stories that have shaped you. Your journey has illuminated the past and holds the promise of a future where the echoes of your ancestors' experiences continue to resonate.

GLOSSARY OF GENEALOGY TERMS

Genealogy research comes with its own unique terminology that can sometimes be overwhelming, especially for those new to the field. This glossary provides explanations for key terms and concepts that you'll encounter on your African American genealogy journey.

Ancestry: The lineage of individuals or families traced backward in time.

Census Records: Official government surveys of the population, conducted at regular intervals, that provide valuable demographic information about individuals and households.

DNA Testing: The analysis of an individual's DNA to gain insights into their genetic makeup, heritage, and potential familial connections.

GEDCOM: Genealogical Data Communication format, a standard file format used to exchange genealogical data between different software programs.

Lineage: The sequence of ancestors and descendants in a direct line of descent.

Oral History: The transmission of historical information, stories, and traditions through spoken accounts passed down from one generation to another.

Pedigree Chart: A graphical representation of an individual's direct ancestors, often presented in a tree-like structure.

Primary Source: Original records or documents created at the time of an event, providing firsthand information about that event.

Secondary Source: Records or documents that were created after an event occurred and may not provide firsthand information.

Slave Records: Documents related to the lives and status of enslaved individuals, often found in plantation records, wills, and other historical documents.

Transcription: The process of converting handwritten or printed text into a digital or typed format for easier reading and analysis.

Y-DNA: A type of DNA passed down from father to son along the direct paternal line, used to trace male ancestry.

Mitochondrial DNA: A type of DNA passed from mother to all her children, used to trace maternal ancestry.

Autosomal DNA: The non-sex chromosomes that contain genetic information from both parents and can provide insights into recent family connections.

Brick Wall: A point in genealogy research where progress is hindered due to lack of information or difficulty in finding records.

Descendant: A person's child, grandchild, great-grandchild, and so on.

Ancestor: A person's parent, grandparent, great-grandparent, and so on.

Research Log: A record of your research activities, including sources consulted, information found, and next steps.

Archival Repository: A place where historical documents, records, and artifacts are stored, often maintained by libraries, archives, or historical societies.

Collaborative Genealogy: The practice of working with other researchers to share information, collaborate on projects, and solve genealogical mysteries together.

Documentation: Keeping track of sources and evidence used in your research to ensure accuracy and credibility.

This glossary serves as a reference to help you navigate the terminology of genealogy research. As you delve deeper into your African American ancestry, understanding these terms will enable you to communicate effectively, make informed decisions, and successfully navigate the complexities of genealogical exploration.

CONCLUSION: A TAPESTRY OF HERITAGE AND DISCOVERY

As you conclude this journey through African American genealogy, you stand at the crossroads of the past and the present, holding in your hands a tapestry woven from the threads of history, resilience, and identity. Your dedication to uncovering the hidden stories of your ancestors has illuminated the shadows of the past and breathed life into names long forgotten. With each record unearthed, each connection made, and each story shared, you have become a guardian of a legacy that stretches across generations.

Through the pages of this book, you've embarked on a transformative quest—one that transcends dates and names, and reaches into the heart of human experience. You've navigated the challenges of tracing African American ancestry, from the complexities of slave records to the revelations of DNA testing. You've explored the landscapes of oral history, census data, and vital records, piecing together the puzzle of your family's narrative. Along the way, you've celebrated triumphs, confronted contradictions, and embraced the stories of resilience that define your heritage.

Remember that your journey does not end here. The path of genealogy is one of infinite discovery, where each revelation leads to more questions and new avenues to explore. As you continue your exploration of African American ancestry, know that your efforts contribute to a broader understanding of history—a history that is rich, diverse, and interconnected. Your journey extends an invitation to future generations to explore their roots, celebrate their heritage, and stand on the shoulders of those who came before.

May your discoveries continue to ignite the flame of curiosity, deepen your appreciation for the lives that have shaped yours, and inspire you to pass on the torch of exploration. In every story you uncover, in every ancestor you honor, you breathe life into the past and contribute to the story of humanity itself. Your journey is a testament to the enduring power of connection, the resilience of spirit, and the infinite potential of discovery.

APPENDIX A: RESOURCES FOR AFRICAN AMERICAN GENEALOGY RESEARCH

Embarking on an African American genealogy journey requires access to a range of resources that can guide your research, provide context, and connect you with a supportive community. This appendix is a comprehensive compilation of resources that can serve as valuable tools throughout your exploration.

Online Databases and Websites

1. **Ancestry.com**: Offers extensive collections of census records, vital records, military records, and more.
2. **FamilySearch**: A vast online repository of genealogical records, including digitized historical documents and family trees.
3. **AfriGeneas**: A resource and community dedicated to African American genealogy, with databases, forums, and helpful guides.
4. **African American Genealogy Group**: A Facebook group where researchers can share findings, ask questions, and connect with others.
5. **Slave Voyages Database**: Provides information on the transatlantic slave trade, aiding in tracing enslaved ancestors' origins.

Archives and Libraries

1. **National Archives and Records Administration (NARA)**: Houses federal records, including census data, military records, and historical documents.

2. **Library of Congress**: Offers access to manuscripts, newspapers, photographs, and more, contributing to a deeper understanding of history.
3. **Allen County Public Library's Genealogy Center**: Contains an extensive collection of African American genealogy resources, both online and in-person.

African American Historical and Genealogical Societies

1. **Afro-American Historical and Genealogical Society (AAHGS)**: Provides research guidance, educational resources, and a supportive community.
2. **Black Genealogy Research Group**: Offers resources, webinars, and forums for those researching African American genealogy.
3. **African American Civil War Soldiers Database**: Focuses on African American soldiers who fought in the Civil War.

DNA Testing Services

1. **AncestryDNA**: Offers insights into your ethnicity and potential DNA matches with other users.
2. **23andMe**: Provides ancestry reports and health-related insights based on your DNA.
3. **MyHeritage DNA**: Offers ethnic origins analysis and DNA matching to discover potential relatives.

Educational and Community Initiatives

1. **PBS "Finding Your Roots"**: A TV series that explores the genealogy of well-known individuals, shedding light on African American history.

2. **African American History Month**: An annual observance in February with events, discussions, and educational resources.

Books and Publications

1. **"Black Genesis: A Resource Book for African-American Genealogy" by James M. Rose**: A comprehensive guide to African American genealogy research.
2. **"The African American Family's Guide to Tracing Our Roots" by Roland C. Barksdale-Hall**: Offers practical advice and insights for researching African American ancestry.

Local Historical Societies and Archives

Explore the resources available in the regions where your ancestors lived. Local societies, archives, and libraries may hold valuable records and information.

Remember that the world of genealogy is continually evolving, with new resources and discoveries being made regularly. Stay open to exploring new avenues, connecting with fellow researchers, and sharing your findings to contribute to the rich tapestry of African American history.

APPENDIX B: SAMPLE TEMPLATES: FAMILY TREE CHARTS, RESEARCH LOGS, AND ORAL HISTORY INTERVIEW QUESTIONS

A research log is an essential tool for keeping track of your genealogical investigations. It helps you organize your findings, track sources, and stay focused on your research goals. Below is a sample research log template that you can adapt to your own research needs.

Date	Source	Information Found	Next Steps
2023-03-01	Ancestry.com Census 1870	Found John Smith (age 35) and family in Philadelphia, PA	Cross-reference with marriage records
2023-03-05	Philadelphia Archives	Located marriage record for John Smith and Mary Johnson in 1858	Check for birth records for John and Mary
2023-03-10	Family interview	Grandma mentioned a family Bible with birth dates	Inquire with relatives about the Bible's location
2023-03-15	DNA Matches	Connected with potential cousins with the surname Johnson	Research Johnson family history
2023-03-20	Local Library	Found an article in a historical newspaper about John Smith's store	Research local history and business directories

Family Group Sheet Template

A family group sheet is a document that provides a structured overview of a nuclear family unit. It includes essential information about each family member and their relationships. Use the template below to create family group sheets for each family unit you research.

Family Group Sheet

```
Husband's Name:          Birthdate:          Birthplace:
Wife's   Maiden   Name:                      Birthdate:
Birthplace:

Marriage Date:           Marriage Place:

Children  (List  all  children  with  birthdates  and
birthplaces):
Name:          Birthdate:          Birthplace:
Name:          Birthdate:          Birthplace:
Name:          Birthdate:          Birthplace:

Sources (Census, Vital Records, etc.):
Source: Description of Information Found
Source: Description of Information Found
```

DNA Testing Companies

Here are some well-known DNA testing companies that offer different types of genetic testing for genealogical purposes:

1. **AncestryDNA**: Offers autosomal DNA testing to provide insights into ethnicity and potential matches.
2. **23andMe**: Provides ancestry reports, health insights, and the option to connect with genetic relatives.
3. **MyHeritage DNA**: Offers ethnicity estimates and DNA matching for potential relatives.

Sample Letter for Requesting Records

When contacting archives, libraries, or institutions to request specific records, a well-written letter can be effective. Customize the sample letter below to suit your needs.

```
[Your Name]
[Your Address]
[City, State, ZIP]
[Email Address]
[Phone Number]
[Date]

[Recipient's Name]
[Institution's Name]
[Institution's Address]
[City, State, ZIP]

Dear [Recipient's Name],

I hope this letter finds you well. I am writing to request
assistance in locating specific records related to my genealogical
research. I am particularly interested in [provide details about the
records you are seeking, such as census records, marriage
certificates, etc.].

I understand that your institution may have valuable resources
that could shed light on my family history. I would greatly appreciate
any guidance you can offer regarding the availability of these
records and the steps I need to take to access them.

If there are any fees associated with accessing or obtaining
copies of these records, please let me know. I am more than willing
to cover any costs necessary to further my research.

Thank you in advance for your time and consideration. I am
enthusiastic about the possibility of uncovering more about my
ancestors and their stories. I look forward to hearing from you soon.

Sincerely,
[Your Name]
```

These appendixes provide practical tools and templates to assist you in your African American genealogy research. Adapt and utilize them to support your journey in gathering information, organizing your findings, and reaching out to institutions for record requests.

Unveiling Roots: Tracing African American Ancestry and Slave Records" continues Penelope Green's commitment to helping individuals discover their heritage and connect with their past. Through comprehensive research strategies, insightful storytelling, and a focus on the unique challenges faced by African American families, this book aims to empower readers with the tools they need to uncover their lineage and honor their ancestors' legacies.

www.ingramcontent.com/pod-product-compliance
Lightning Source LLC
Chambersburg PA
CBHW060256030426
42335CB00014B/1732